HAP PALMER
HOMEMADE BAND

HAP PALMER
HOMEMADE

BAND

SONGS TO SING
INSTRUMENTS TO MAKE

Crown Publishers, Inc.
New York

Published by Crown Publishers, Inc., a Random House company,
225 Park Avenue South, New York, New York 10003

CROWN is a trademark of Crown Publishers, Inc.
Manufactured in the United States of America

Library of Congress Cataloging-in-Publication Data
Palmer, Hap. 1942–   Homemade band / Hap Palmer : illustrations by Linda
Bourke. p. cm.
Summary: Provides lyrics for nine original songs and instructions for making
simple instruments to accompany each song. 1. Musical instruments–
Construction–Juvenile. 2. Children's songs. [1. Songs. 2. Musical instruments–
Construction.] I. Bourke, Linda, ill. II. Title.
MT740.P28 1990   782.42'0268–dc20   90-37464
                                                          CIP
                                                          AC MN

ISBN 0-517-58022-5 (book and cassette)
     0-517-57597-3 (lib. bdg.)
10 9 8 7 6 5 4 3 2 1
First Edition

Making music is lots of fun when you play along on your own instruments. You don't have to go out and buy expensive drums, guitars, or maracas, either. Using household items, you can easily create super-duper musical instruments yourself! Always ask a parent or adult supervisor's permission first, of course. It's smart to be safe before you begin any crafts project. And it's always polite to ask if you may borrow any of Mom's or Dad's supplies!

Each song in this book will sound great when you accompany it with your special musical instruments that you've made at home. Get your friends to join in and you, too, can have your very own homemade band!

Hap Palmer

Michael LeRoy

Homemade Band

Here's a little story 'bout a homemade band
Some friends of mine made by hand.
Sally found a bolt and she hit it with a spoon,
Then she smiled and sang this tune.
  She cried "oooh– aaah–" and everyone could understand
  That Sally was havin' fun with the homemade band.

Jackie found some bottle caps
And tacked them to a piece of wood.
He shook that thing with a jing-a-ling
And it was really sounding good.
  He cried "oooh– aaah–" and everyone could understand
  That Jackie was havin' fun with the homemade band.

Steve and Susan saved several soda cans,
And empty plastic bottles, too.
They dropped in little beads, dried beans, or rice,
And made some shakers good as new.

Rosa found some plywood scraps
And strips of wood that weren't too thick.
With glue she made a hollow block
And hit it with a little stick.
    She cried "oooh– aaah–" and everyone could understand
    That Rosa was havin' fun with the homemade band.

Ollie eyed an ordinary oatmeal box
And fished it from the kitchen trash.
He set it on the floor with some pots and pans
And played a rhythm–boom, boom, bash.

Playing all together you could hear their sound
Ringing all across the land.
People came from everywhere to listen to
The rhythm of the homemade band.
    They cried "oooh– aaah–" and everyone could understand
    That my friends were havin' fun with the homemade band.

I'm a Little Woodblock

I'm a little woodblock—tick, tock, tick.
Pick me up and tap me with a stick.

I'm a little bolt that you can ring.
Strike me with a spoon and hear me sing.

Oh, I'm a tambourine that you can shake.
Won't you let me share the sound I make?

We're a friendly pair of slender sticks.
Together we go click, click, click.

I'm a little shaker with one wish:
Shake me, please, and hear me swish.

Oh, we're the instruments that you can make.
Play us all at once–just tap and shake.

Get ready to tap your woodblock to the tune of "I'm a Little Teapot." A woodblock can easily be made once you get an adult to help you locate some screw eyes and a piece of wood. Here's how:

WOOD
SPOO

SHOE
LACE

SCREW
EYES

WOODEN
BLOCK

Simple Block

Using screw eyes or small nails, tie a string or shoelace to the end of a small scrap of wood so it can swing freely. Try different sizes of wood–whatever is handy will do. Hit it with a wooden stick, a wooden spoon, or a string-padded mallet. Hit the block in different places–bottom edge, top edge, middle. Which sound do you like the best?

Hollow Block

This block has a surprisingly pleasing, resonant sound. It is made from scraps of 1/4″ plywood and 3/4″ square pine.

PLYWOOD SCRAPS

WOOD GLUE

RUBBER BANDS

PINE SCRAPS

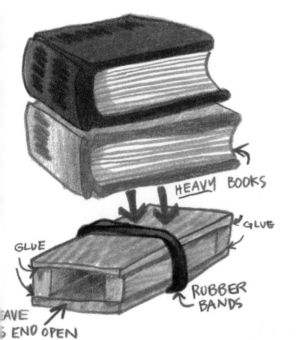

HEAVY BOOKS

GLUE

GLUE

RUBBER BANDS

LEAVE ONE END OPEN

Glue three pieces of 3/4″ square pine on top of one piece of 1/4″ plywood so that each piece runs along an edge. Leave one edge open. Then glue a second piece of 1/4″ plywood on top to form a hollow block. Use good-quality wood glue. Put the block under weight (books, a rock, etc.) or pressure (rubber bands, a C-clamp) and allow to dry overnight.

Put screw eyes in one end and hang the block on a string or shoelace. There is no exact size the block should be. Generally, the larger the block, the lower the sound; the smaller the block, the higher the sound. The block pictured is 4″ x 8″.

Slow and Fast Song

Slowly, slowly,
Playing slowly,
Slowly as snails go sliding by,
Slowly as clouds drift through the sky.

Faster, faster, playing faster
With a rapid, rhythmic clatter.
Quickly, quickly, clicking, clanging,
Clacking, smacking, booming, banging,
Like a charging cheetah chasing
Frightened rabbits, running, racing.
Listen to us madly play
In our very fastest way!

Slowly, slowly,
Playing slowly,
Slowly as leaves turn brown in the fall,
Slowly as turtles move when they crawl.

Faster, faster, playing faster
With a rapid, rhythmic clatter.
Quickly, quickly, clicking, clanging,
Clacking, smacking, booming, banging,
Like a fly darts through the flowers,
Like a jet on super power.
Listen to us madly play
In our very fastest way!

Pots and Pans, Cartons and Cans

Try striking different things with different mallets. Soon you will discover the sounds you like best. Here are some things you can try hitting:

Metal frying pan
Metal saucepan
Plastic wastebasket

Empty coffee can
Oatmeal box

These different drums will help you keep the beat, whether you're drumming at a snail's pace or as fast as a charging cheetah!

All you need are some mallets, and the kitchen becomes a treasure chest of sounds. A collection of different mallets will give you a variety of sounds. Here are some you can try:

WOODEN SPOON

Use as is for a great all-purpose mallet.

WOODEN STICK

Use a chopstick, or the handle of a wooden spoon.

STRING-WRAPPED MALLET

For a softer, gonglike sound, wrap string tightly around one end of a stick to form a ball-shaped end.

PADDED MALLET

Stuff some of the open end of a sock up into itself so it feels padded, and then put it over the bowl end of a wooden spoon. Hold it on with a tight elastic band or with a piece of string tied tightly.

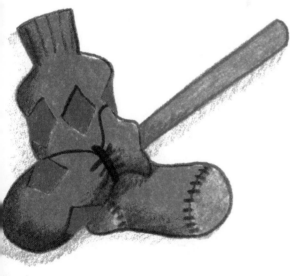

METAL SPOON

If you like loud, clanging sounds, this is the mallet for you!

Soft and Loud Song

Tiny raindrops falling softly
On the window pane.
Baby's sleeping warm and safely
Sheltered from the rain.

Boom! Crash!
Thunder and lightning.
Jagged flashes pierce the skies.
Boom! Crash!
Rumbling so loudly,
Little baby wakes and cries.

Rocking, rocking, gently calming
Baby on my knees.
Clouds are passing, last drips falling
Softly from the trees.
(Repeat.)

Play softly when you hear soft music and loudly when you hear the thundering sounds in the middle verse of The Soft and Loud Song. Gently click sticks for soft sounds. Pot-lid cymbals are terrific for making booming and crashing noises. But you can use any instruments you like to play this song.

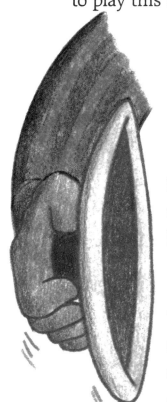

Pot-Lid Cymbals

Pick two lids about the same size with easy-to-hold handles. Hold one in each hand and brush them back and forth on each other.

or

Use just one lid and hit it with a metal spoon for a loud crashing sound. Use a string-wrapped mallet and hit the inside edge of the lid for a pleasant gong-like sound. Try different kinds of mallets and strike the lid in different places. Which sound do you like the best?

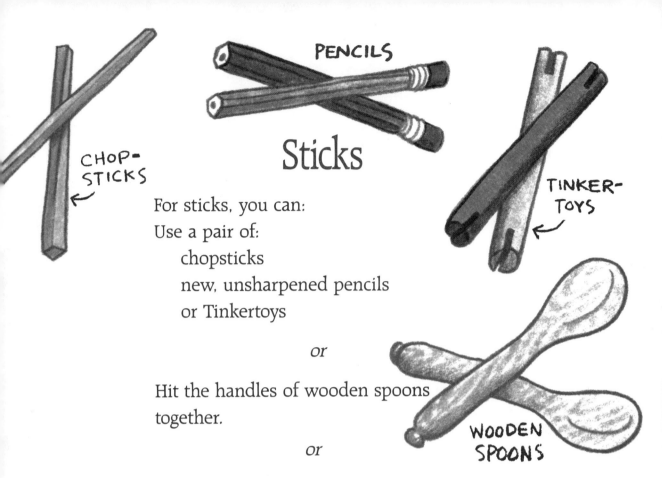

Sticks

PENCILS

CHOP-STICKS

TINKER-TOYS

WOODEN SPOONS

For sticks, you can:
Use a pair of:
    chopsticks
    new, unsharpened pencils
    or Tinkertoys

or

Hit the handles of wooden spoons together.

or

Get some hardwood dowels from a hardware store or lumber yard—they often come in 3-foot lengths. Have an adult cut off 1-foot sections. Thinner sticks have a clearer, higher, softer sound. Thicker sticks have a louder, fuller sound.

or

Have an adult saw off 1-foot sections of an old broom or mop handle.

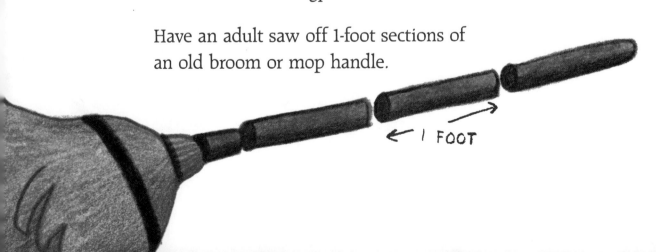

← 1 FOOT →

Old MacDonald's Band

Old MacDonald had a band, Eee-yi-eee-yi-oh,
And kitty cat played kazoo, Eee-yi-eee-yi-oh.
With a toot toot here and a toot toot there,
Here a toot, there a toot, everywhere a toot toot.
Old MacDonald had a band, Eee-yi-eee-yi-oh.

Old MacDonald had a band, Eee-yi-eee-yi-oh,
And Brahma bull played the bells, Eee-yi-eee-yi-oh.
With a jingle here and a jingle there,
Here a jing, there a jing, everywhere a jingle.
Old MacDonald had a band, Eee-yi-eee-yi-oh.

Old MacDonald had a band, Eee-yi-eee-yi-oh,
And pony played the pot-lid cymbals, Eee-yi-eee-yi-oh.
With a clang clang here and a clang clang there,
Here a clang, there a clang, everywhere a clang, clang.
Old MacDonald had a band, Eee-yi-eee-yi-oh.

Old MacDonald had a band, Eee-yi-eee-yi-oh,
And cows and chickens played the shakers, Eee-yi-eee-yi-oh.
With a shake shake here and a shake shake there,
Here a shake, there a shake, everywhere a shake shake.
Old MacDonald had a band, Eee-yi-eee-yi-oh.

Old MacDonald had a band, Eee-yi-eee-yi-oh,
And everybody played at once, Eee-yi-eee-yi-oh.
With a noise noise here, and a noise noise there,
Here a noise, there a noise, everywhere a noise, noise.
Old MacDonald had a band, Eee-yi-eee-yi-oh.

"Old MacDonald's Band" is another old favorite we've turned around. Old MacDonald's crazy band plays instruments made from objects you can probably find right in your own home. Shakers are particularly easy to make and can sound every bit as good as real maracas!

Shakers

Here are some "ecology shakers" you can make by recycling household containers. Dried peas, beans, or rice can be used for noisemakers. You can also use seeds or small pebbles.

PLASTIC JAR SHAKER

Drop noisemakers inside the jar and screw the top on tightly. Try a few noisemakers, then try lots of noisemakers. Which sound do you like the best? If you use small plastic bottles, you can make two and play one in each hand. For a different sound, try a large plastic jug.

SODA OR JUICE CAN SHAKER

Wash out the inside of the can and be sure it is dry before you put anything in it. Drop noisemakers inside, then tape the opening shut with masking tape.

BANDAGE CAN SHAKER

Put noisemakers into the can and clamp the lid down tight. It should catch, but if it seems to open easily, you can put a little tape around the top to hold it shut.

You can also make shakers with plastic film containers or small boxes. Can you think of other kinds of containers? What else could you use for noisemakers?

Bells

HAVE AN ADULT
MAKE
A HOLE
WITH A
NAIL

LARGE
KNOTS

HANG
A SCREW
INSIDE

TIN CAN BELL

Have an adult punch a hole in the top of an emptied soup can. Tie a string around a screw or nail, leaving long ends on the string. Thread the string through the hole in the can and tie a fat knot at the end to keep the string from sliding through the hole.

Holiday packages are often decorated with bells. Instead of throwing them out, here are several ways to use them:

BODY BELLS

Run the end of a piece of yarn or string through the loop on a bell. Then tie the string around your wrist. You can make several and put them on your wrists and ankles and be your own band. If you have extra bells, put a few on each string to make more of a jingle.

JINGLE BELLS

String the jingle bells on a piece of yarn and tie it into a loop. Hold the loop and shake.

JINGLE STICK

Using string or pipe cleaners, tie the bells to the upper half of a stick of wood. Hold the bottom and shake.

Drivin' Down the Highway

They'll be drivin' down the highway when they come–*beep, beep.*
They'll be drivin' down the highway when they come–*beep, beep.*
They'll be drivin' down the highway,
                              Then come turnin' in the driveway.
They'll be drivin' down the highway when they come–
Beep, beep.

Grandpa Bill will ring the bell when he comes–*ding, dong.*
Grandpa Bill will ring the bell when he comes–*ding, dong.*
Grandpa Bill will ring the bell,
                              We'll say "My, you're lookin' well!"
Grandpa Bill will ring the bell when he comes–
Ding, dong, beep, beep.

Grandma Jean will jingle keys when she comes–*jing, jang.*
Grandma Jean will jingle keys when she comes–*jing, jang.*
Grandma Jean will jingle keys,
                              Bouncing baby on her knees.
Grandma Jean will jingle keys when she comes–
Jing, jang, ding, dong, beep, beep.

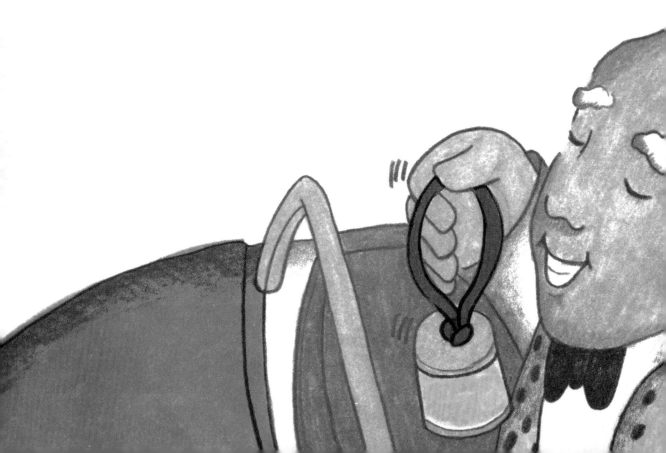

Sister Rose will tap her toes when she comes–*tap, tap.*
Sister Rose will tap her toes when she comes–*tap, tap.*
Sister Rose will tap her toes

                    When we play the tune she chose.

Sister Rose will tap her toes when she comes–
Tap, tap, jing, jang, ding, dong, beep, beep.

Uncle Dan will bang the pans when he comes–*clang, clang.*
Uncle Dan will bang the pans when he comes–*clang, clang.*
Uncle Dan will bang the pans
                    And some empty coffee cans.
Uncle Dan will bang the pans when he comes–
Clang, clang, tap, tap, jing, jang, ding, dong, beep, beep.

Cousin Clem will clap his hands when he comes–*clap, clap.*
Cousin Clem will clap his hands when he comes–*clap, clap.*
Cousin Clem will clap his hands
                    While he's singing with the band.
Cousin Clem will clap his hands when he comes–
Clap, clap, clang, clang, tap, tap, jing, jang, ding, dong, beep, beep.
They'll be drivin' down the highway when they come.

You'll probably recognize the melody to "Drivin' Down the Highway"! It's sung to the tune of "She'll Be Comin' 'Round the Mountain." But this version gives you plenty of opportunities to make some funny noises. You can just sing the noises *or* you can play an instrument. Try the "Beep beep" on a kazoo. Jingle keys along with Grandma Jean. All you need are ordinary house keys–the more the better–and a wire coat hanger.

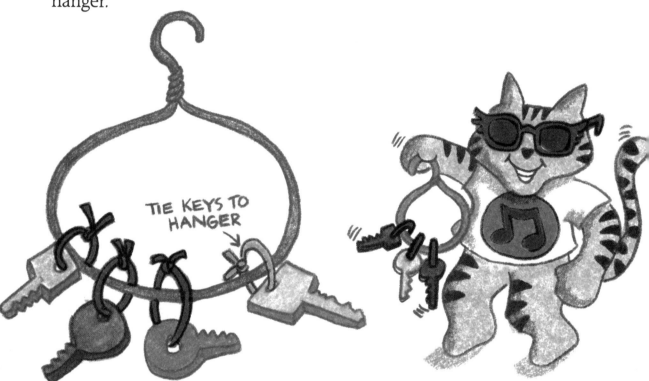

TIE KEYS TO HANGER

Make a metal coat hanger round by pulling it out on the bottom. Run a piece of string through each key and loop the string over the wire hanger. Tie the string, making sure it is long enough and loose enough to swing freely. When you have all the keys tied on, hold the hanger by the hook end and shake.

Kazoo

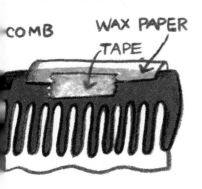

COMB — WAX PAPER — TAPE

COMB AND PAPER KAZOO

Tape a piece of wax paper or tissue paper over the end of a small pocket comb. Put your lips directly against the paper side. Now, hum a little tune. Try humming into the other side of the comb. Which sound do you like the best?

CARDBOARD TUBE KAZOO

Use an empty cardboard roll from paper towels or toilet paper. Put wax paper or tissue paper over one end of the roll–enough to cover the end and come about an inch down the sides. Tape the paper down tight. Put your mouth right up into the open end of the tube, and hum into it. The wax paper will vibrate and make a buzzing sound.

MAKE A HOLE HERE

CARDBOARD TUBE

WAX PAPER

TAPE OR RUBBER BAND

Stick Dance

Let's do the stick dance:
    You tap it and you twirl it.
Let's do the stick dance:
    You swish it and you swirl it,
Shake it and roll it,
    Balance and hold it.
Create a little stick dance–
    It's easy to do.

Pretend to ride it,
    Then set it down and slide it,
Jump it and jiggle,
    Then wave it as you wiggle.
Now move your own way,
    Have fun and just play,
Create a little stick dance–
    It's easy to do.

Let's do the stick dance:
    You tap it and you twirl it.
Let's do the stick dance:
    You swish it and you swirl it.
Now move your own way,
    Have fun and just play,
Create a little stick dance–
    It's easy to do.

You don't always need a partner when you want to get up and dance.
Use your imagination and a stick and you can create a dance all your
own. Play it safe, though, and use a cardboard mailing tube or golf
club as your partner. If you do use a real stick, put cloth and tape over
each end.

Play and Rest

Play two beats and then rest two beats.
   (X means play and □ means rest.)
   X X □ □ X X □ □ X X □ □ X X □ □
   X X □ □ X X □ □

Play four beats and then rest four beats.
   X X X X □ □ □ □ X X X X □ □ □ □
   X X X X □ □ □ □

Play three beats and then rest one beat.
   X X X □ X X X □ X X X □ X X X □
   X X X □ X X X □

Play one beat and then rest three beats.
   X □ □ □ X □ □ □ X □ □ □ X □ □ □
   X □ □ □ X □ □ □

Play and rest anytime you want to.
Play and rest anytime you want to.

You can use any instrument at all as accompaniment for "Play and Rest." Bottles will make soft whistling sounds like a flute. Pucker your lips up like you do when you whistle, and then whistle across the open mouth of the bottle. Keep trying until you get a sound you like. If you use a bunch of different-sized bottles, or fill some same-sized bottles with different amounts of water, you can blow lots of different notes.

Old-Fashioned Rock and Roll

Clappin' my hands with a rock and roll band,
    Just feelin' happy and free.
Tappin' my sticks with a ricky tick tick
    To the rhythm and the melody.
Bangin' these pans every way I can
    With spirit and energy.
Just playin' along with a good old-fashioned rock and roll song.

Chorus:
Singin' "Dance to the music."
    Leavin' my troubles and worries behind
Singin' "Dance to the music."
    All you gotta do is have a good time.

Clangin' my spoons to a happy-time tune
    That's puttin' everyone at ease.
Rattlin' little rocks in an oatmeal box,
    Playin' any way I please.
Shakin' jars with beans, or a tambourine,
    Or jinglin' my daddy's keys.
Just playin' along with a good old-fashioned rock and roll song.

(Repeat chorus.)

We shimmy and sway as we sing and play
    With the songs of yesterday.
Just playin' along with a good old-fashioned rock and roll song.

A tambourine makes a great rhythm instrument. Collect some bottle caps and a glass jar, and you can make your own at home. Here's how:

Bottle Cap Tambourines

JAR TAMBOURINE

Drop a bunch of bottle caps into a small jar. Put enough bottle caps in the jar so that they will make a nice jingle but still have enough room to move around. Screw the lid on tight. Shake it gently for a soft, jingly sound.

STICK TAMBOURINE

For this tambourine you need only two bottle caps. Have an adult punch a hole in the center of each bottle cap. This can be done with a medium-size nail. Ask an adult to attach the bottle cap to a slender piece of wood using a smaller nail (so the cap can ring freely). A piece 1/2" square by 6" long is ideal, but any size will do.

For a louder, clearer jingling sound:
    Remove any plastic or cork which lines
        the inside of the bottle cap.
    Place metal washers between the
        two bottle caps.

Bolts make a dandy ringing sound that's perfect for rock and roll.

Bolts

Use a large eyebolt. Loop a shoelace or piece of string through the eye of the bolt so it can hang freely. Strike the bolt with a metal spoon handle for a beautiful ringing sound much like the sound from a triangle or chime.

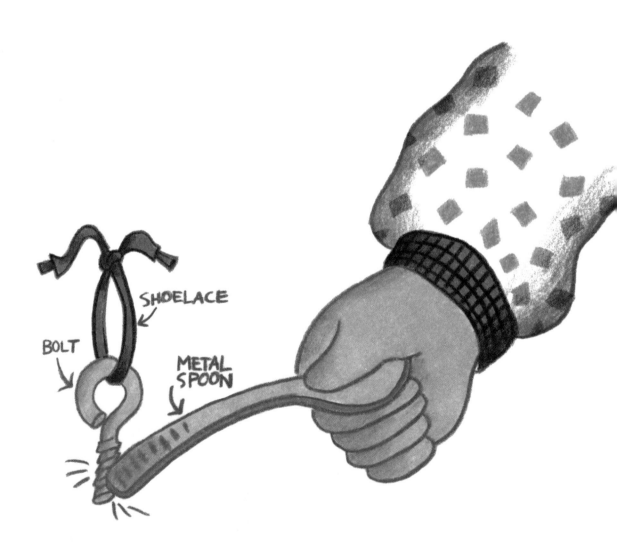

SHOELACE

BOLT

METAL
SPOON